SUPER SIGHT-READING SECRETS

Howard Richman

*An innovative, step-by-step program
for keyboard* players of all levels*

Revised 3rd Edition

786.23
R412

*Adaptable to other instruments

Sound Feelings Publishing

Newhall, California

SOUND FEELINGS PUBLISHING
24266 Walnut Street
Newhall, California 91321
U.S.A.

Richman, Howard
    Super Sight-Reading Secrets
    1. Sight-Reading (Music).
    2. Piano — Instruction and Study.
    3. Music — Instruction and Study.
    4. Music — Manuals, Text-books, etc.
    5. Sythesizer (Musical Instrument) Methods.
    6. Educational Psychology.
    I. Title

Library of Congress Catalog Card Number: 85-90522
ISBN: 0-9615963-0-9 Softcover

Typesetting & Layout by Mark Coniglio
Cover Illustration by Brenda Chapman
Music Typesetting by Bin Wang

Manufactured in the United States of America
Revised 3rd Edition

CONTENTS

Preface

That was incredible... Now, will you play *this* for me?"
(silence)
"Uh... I don't... I'm sorry, I'm not a good *s i g h t - r e a d e r.*"

Sound familiar? I can't say how many times the above scenario repeated itself with me. I could play Chopin *Etudes* faster that the speed of light, but couldn't read musical comedy tunes at parties. *Embarrassing* is an understatement. Out of desperation, in 1975, I resolved to improve my sight-reading so that I could truly become a well-rounded musician.

After much observing, imitating, dissecting, analyzing, experimenting, and practicing, I not only have exceeded the ability of my former sight-reading idols, but I've been able to show others how to do the same. This book represents the best of *what works.* It doesn't matter if you play classical, jazz, rock, for fun, for money — or whether your instrument is the piano, guitar or flute. There *is* something more you can do besides "just practice and it will get better" (the typical suggestion given by many music teachers when asked how to improve sight-reading ability).

You are about to discover this for yourself.

Howard Richman

1 Introduction

What comes naturally to one musician may be insurmountable to another. Each of us has a "natural" ability in one aspect of music. The ones who become successful usually must find ways to *artificially* boost their weaknesses until they too are natural.

Is your strong point technique, hearing, expression, appreciation, reading? Speaking for myself, I had a natural affinity for each of them except for reading. This clearly restricted my ability on the whole. As my reading improved, I noticed a respective improvement in the other areas. This was the gift I gave to myself!

The problem that most of us have is that we often *ignore* our weaknesses. It is not uncommon to see someone who already has a great technique *practicing* technique for three hours a day; or to watch someone who has a great ear rely on this gift/crutch to excess. It is the rare person who sees his or her weakness and commits full attention to *that.* The reason I bring this up is because *you* are going to have to do the work here. Hopefully this book will bombard you with ideas, inspiration, and a plan of action, but *you* are the one who must **practice**.

How long before you reach your goal depends on 1) how quickly you learn, and 2) how serious you are about doing the drills. Fifteen minutes every day is superior to two hours once a week. Regularity is the key. The actual time per practice session depends on your schedule. A thorough mastery of the core drills alone (Chapters 5 & 6) can take anywhere between three months to four years. You must always be patient and go at your own pace.

Super Sight-Reading Secrets is written for keyboard (piano, synthesizer, organ, harpsichord) players but is easily adaptable to players of other instruments as well (see Chapter 10). It is also for musicians of all levels; the beginner,[*] the professional, and anyone in between. The drills are progressive. Just cut in where you begin to be challenged and go from there.

[*] Young beginners will need help from their teacher.

2 The Psychology of Sight-Reading

"If we do not open our eyes, we will not see." This is an obvious statement, but think about it for a moment in less literal terms. How many times have you had your eyes open but *still* missed something important?

To sight-read we must be an open vessel. We must be a sponge — ready to soak up information. The great inhibitor here, you will find, is our own thoughts! Worries, doubts, expectations, fears, distractions… Our mind becomes cluttered or blocked. This weakens its receptive faculties. In other words, the more brain-power we use to *think*, the less we will have available to take in new information. All of a sudden, we then have a closed vessel.

Clearly understand, I'm not saying *not* to think. What I am suggesting is that it may be more than coincidental that "most good sight-readers can't perfect a piece, and most good perfectionists can't sight read." I believe it is good to be able to do both, and therefore good to cultivate two separate brain processes: 1) *thought & analysis* and 2) *gathering data*. These might be compared to the modes of a computer.

When we work on a piece, thought and analysis is needed. To sight-read, we should be in the "gathering data" mode. Psychologically, we can help ourselves by *emulating* the naturally good sight-reader when we sight-read. This person might make some mistakes, but he or she wouldn't be bothered by them. Good sight-readers won't waste a second of valuable *thought-time* on mistakes. Instead, they're off, zooming ahead to soak up more information.

The drills in this book demand a thorough analysis just to understand them. But when you take your new ability and actually test it out, open not only your eyes but your *brain.*

3 Basics

The purpose of this chapter is to provide a *needed foundation for what is to follow*. If you are a beginner, this information will be particularly useful, though it must not be taken as a thorough introduction to musical notation, nor as a substitute for private instruction. Advanced players should give a quick skim for any new ideas, then go to the next chapter. (Make sure you can do the **Basic Perception Drills** at the end of the chapter.)

Perceive a minimum of three elements

Written music tells us a minimum of 3 things: **Pitch**, **Rhythm**, and **Fingering**. The **pitch** describes how high or low a note is and is determined by *where* the note is placed on the staff. The **rhythm** describes how long a note lasts and is determined by *what* the note looks like. The **fingering** may be written in, but is often *implied* by the shape of the phrase. Of course, the composer makes indications for dynamics, tempo, articulation, moods, etc. But these make sense only if the first three steps are mastered.

Conscious effort becomes automatic

Our goal is to at least be able to grasp the pitch, rhythmic and fingering information supplied all at once. The process needed, however, to acquire this ability is to focus on one thing at a time until it becomes automatic. Speaking out loud (verbalizing) is a way to force our conscious thoughts to coincide with our actions. This "locks in" good habits and prepares us for automation (more on this to follow).

Perceiving Pitch Information

1) Learn the names of the notes on the keyboard

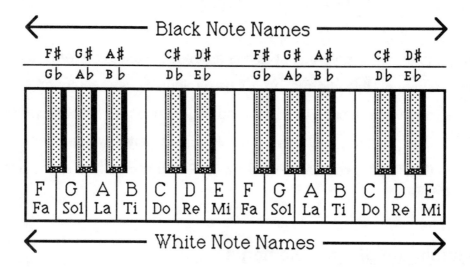

Notice the alternating arrangement of the 2 and 3 black notes. It is in relation to these obvious differences that we establish our points of reference. Each white note has a unique identity as you play in sequence from left to right. When you arrive at a note positioned identically in reference to the blacks as where you started (an *octave*, or eight notes away), it has the same name. This means that there are only 7 different white note names.

For the entire Sight-Reading Program, we will use the Roman alphabet: A-B-C-D-E-F-G to identify the notes. Many people, particularly from countries other than the United States use the *Solmization* system: *Do-Re-Mi-Fa-Sol-La-Ti* (where Do=C). **If you have been trained previously with this latter system, it is perfectly fine if you wish to substitute the syllables for letters in each of the exercises that follow.**

Note Name Drill

Every note to the left of the "2's" (blacks) is a C. Play all the C's on the keyboard up and then down as you say them. (This is probably the only time I will recommend verbalizing *with* the activity rather than before it.) Use the left hand for the lower notes and the right hand for the higher notes. Repeat this on all the white notes. The repeated saying of each note encourages a quick memorization. The up and down aspect of this drill encourages basic eye-hand coordination.

The black notes do not get their own names! Funny, we need them in order to identify the white notes, yet *their* identity is based on the identity of the white notes. Every black note can be referred to as a sharp (♯) or a flat (♭). A black note to the right of a white is a sharp. A black note to the left of a white note is a flat. So, C♯ and D♭ are the same note! (See keyboard diagram.)

2) Learn the names of the notes as they are written

Pitches on the keyboard are represented by their position on the staff:

They can be placed on a line or a space (between two lines).

The **Treble Clef,** 𝄞 , is for instruments that play in the upper register (flute, violin, etc.). The **Bass Clef,** 𝄢 , is for instruments that play in the lower register (tuba, string bass, etc.).

The range of a keyboard will encompass *both* of these registers. This is why piano music is written with 2 staves, connected by a brace:

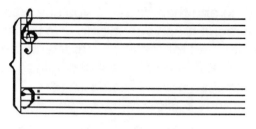

The Grand Staff

These are read from left to right, simultaneously. The right hand usually plays notes in the upper staff and the left hand, the lower. It is important to understand that there is a 90° relationship between what you see and what you play: The higher a note is positioned on the staff, the farther it is to the right on the keyboard, and vice versa.

The **grand staff** represents a central portion of the keyboard and should be understood as a first step to reading music. Notes not included in the staff are represented by **ledger** lines, lines placed above or below the staff (explained soon). The most effective way to learn the names of the notes on the grand staff is to divide it into the four groups of lines and spaces as shown below.

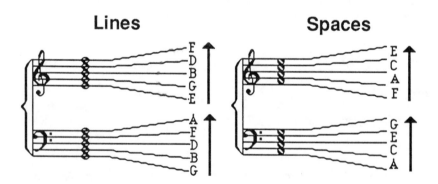

If you read the first space in the Bass Clef, A, and switch to the line, B, above that, and back to space, C, continuing up, line-space-line-space-etc., you've said the alphabet in sequence. With this understanding, you will see that the groups of spaces or lines simply are the letters of the alphabet as you would say them, but skipping every other letter.

Learn each group from the bottom up, as a word. Practice *saying* "E-G-B-D-F,"
"F-A-C-E," etc. Say each group as fast as possible to lock it into the aural memory (as opposed to the visual memory that most people use on these). Do *not*
refer to phrases like "Every Good Boy Deserves Fudge." These devices are
only crutches. This makes it a 2-step process where it should be a 1-step process. (You still have to back-track and acknowledge the first letter of each
word.)

The following examples will assist you in developing the best sequence of
thoughts. Verbalize each step out loud at first, and later to yourself. Finally, the
steps will become so automatic that you will have memorized the notes. In
other words, the following approach is simply a means to an end.

Examples:

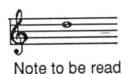

Note to be read

Say: "4th line in the Treble." This tells us which of the four groups we
want. Then say "E-G-B-**D**" and stop on D. (Stop on the one we want.)

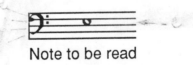

Note to be read

Say: "3rd space in the Bass"... "A-C-**E**." The note is E.

Apply this formula to *Howard's Sight-Reading Drill,* book center.

3) Learn to match what you see with what you play (Even though you
read "D," how do you know which D to play on the keyboard?)

Let's establish a connection between the page and the keyboard.

• Exterior Staff Boundaries

• Keyboard Boundaries

Sitting at "middle D" (see Chapter 5), low G in the left hand and high F in the right hand are the particular notes that are near the hands as they are aimed straight towards the keys at shoulder width. Once you are clear about these reference points (low and high), the exact location of any other note you read can be determined by its relative distance to these notes.

• Ledger Lines

In order to read these, they must be added-to or subtracted-from the nearest one you know.

Example:

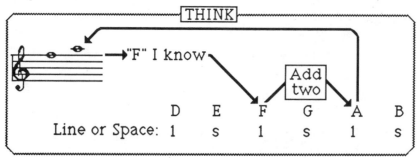

The easiest way to learn to read ledger lines is to learn to count by 3rds rather than by steps. You already know how to do this if you can say the four groups. Just string them together and practice saying them forwards and backwards as a loop, attaching it to itself.

Forwards: E→G→B→D→F→A→C→E

Backwards: E←G←B←D←F←A←C←E

Use the forward loop of 3rds to read upper ledger lines (ascending) and the backward loop for lower ones (descending). You should be able to say either sequence rather fast. If the ledger note in question is on a space, count to the nearest line (by 3rds) and add a step. This, again, is only a means to an end. Eventually you will memorize most ledger lines as well. This exercise will also prove to be helpful for spelling chords, which are constructed by 3rds.

• Interior Staff Boundaries

Notice that between the highest note in the bass staff (A) and the lowest note in the treble (E) there are notes missing. We must add a ledger line for creating "middle C." This is the official divider of the hands. (This doesn't mean that the hands can't ever cross the divider.)

• **Practical Boundaries** (Exterior + "extended" Interior)

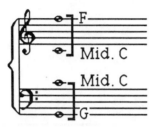

It will be easiest to link what you see with what you play if you are aware of both the exterior and "extended" interior boundaries for each hand. Simply relate the note in question to its relative position within or outside of these boundaries. Then compare this to the keyboard boundaries you've already established.

4) Learn to read accidentals

Accidentals are another name for sharps and flats. The flat (♭) placed before any note means that you play the note 1/2 step below what is written. The sharp (♯) placed before any note means you play the note 1/2 step above what is written. (See **K.O. Drill #4** for 1/2 step explanation.) This "codes" that measure so that any repeated notes will be played with the same alteration automatically. The only way to cancel this code is with the natural sign (♮). Often, an entire piece is coded with a *key signature.* These are sharps or flats at the very beginning which will apply throughout the piece unless further altered.

Perceiving Rhythm Information

1) First let's define some words:

Beat: This is a regularly occurring "pulse" that can be heard or implied.

Tempo: The speed of the pulse.

Measure: (also called "bar") The space between two bar lines. Suggests a unit of time.

Meter: ("time signature") How many beats are in each measure.

Rhythm: Refers to all of the above plus the variation of beats as they are superimposed over the main pulse.

2) Read meters this way: Just say the numerator (how many), then the denominator (what kind).

Examples:

$\frac{4}{4}$ *4* **quarter** notes, or equivalent, in each bar

$\frac{3}{4}$ *3* **quarter** notes, or equivalent, in each bar

$\frac{6}{8}$ *6* **eighth** notes, or equivalent, in each bar

3) The mathematical relationship between note values remains the same even when the unit value changes. The *unit value* is simply the denominator of the meter.

Examples:

$$\eighthnote + \eighthnote = \quarternote \qquad \quarternote + \quarternote = \halfnote$$

$$\eighthnote + \eighthnote = \quarternote \qquad \halfnote + \halfnote = \wholenote$$

In other words, the same two notes will always retain the same relative relationship but may be assigned different values. (This, of course, will alter the value of all the other notes as well.) For example, quarter notes don't always get the beat! Whatever the denominator is — **that** gets the beat.

Example:

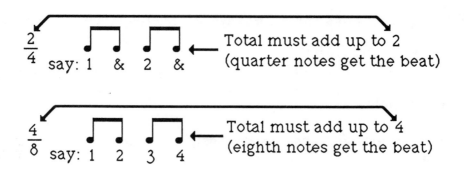

Total must add up to 2 (quarter notes get the beat)

Total must add up to 4 (eighth notes get the beat)

Although the above two examples may appear the same and sound the same, they are counted differently.

Rhythmic Values

(in 4/4 time)

Note	Name	Duration	Equivalent Rest
	Sixteenth	1/4 beat	
	Eighth	1/2 beat	
	Dotted 8th	3/4 beat	
	Quarter	1 beat	
	Dotted Qtr.	1 1/2 beats	
	Half	2 beats	
	Dotted Half	3 beats	
	Whole	4 beats	

Howard's Additive Rhythm Drill

* Begin each note with "one"   * Keep pulse steady
* Play or tap each note while saying the beats

Perceiving Fingering Information

Fingering is based mostly on the context of a note within a passage.

1) First, understand how the fingers are numbered: In sequence from 1 to 5, starting with the thumbs.

2) Often fingering is written in the music but this should never be taken as final. Feel free to change it to suit your hand. It is important, however, to mark these changes with pencil so that you become accustomed to playing exactly what you see.

3) Even if the fingering is not written, it is often implied. Look at the shape of the phrase. Does it go up or down? The goal here is to see how many notes you can play while the hand is in one position. In other words, the less often you need to shift, the more efficient the fingering.

Example: Left hand of measure 39, Chopin *Nocturne,* Op. 32, #1

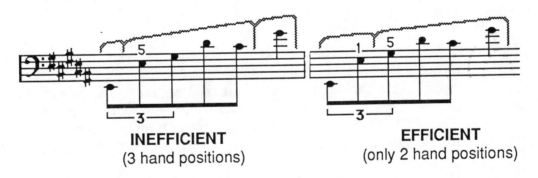

INEFFICIENT
(3 hand positions)

EFFICIENT
(only 2 hand positions)

It is interesting to note that the fingering in the left example is recommended by the editor of a famous edition. Moral: Think for yourself!

Sometimes fingering is selected for power. If you are playing an isolated note marked *ff*, you want a strong finger on it.

Basic Perception Drills

These are basic drills to be done on the simplest of pieces[*] (regardless of your present level) to enhance your perception of the fundamental information all sheet music provides: *pitch, rhythm,* and *fingering.* Since we need fingers to play the pitches (but not necessarily to play rhythms) I've condensed the 3 components into two drills: **Rhythm Alone** and **Pitches and Fingering Alone.** Make sure you can do these easily before going on.

1) Rhythm Alone

- Observe the rhythmic information from the piece.

- Select 2 notes on the keyboard to represent each hand and stay on these. We are not playing the correct pitches here. Instead, we use "dummy" notes. This allows us to devote 100% of our concentration to the rhythmic information.

- TALK! — Verbalize the beats. Say 1, 2, 3, 4 or 1&2&3&4& throughout the entire piece while you play only the rhythmic information indicated by the piece. (The "ands" should be verbalized if eighth notes or faster notes are present. This gives us more verbal points of reference.)

- Begin at a comfortable tempo and gradually increase it until it exceeds the tempo you would take with the correct pitches. This is the "overwork" principle. (If we can run ten miles, one mile will be easy.) Eventually we can add the correct pitches. This will make it more difficult, causing us to slow down — but since we've achieved a faster tempo than necessary, when we slow down, it should be just right. This is a way of planning ahead.

- This is rather tedious and must not be practiced more than two minutes a day. (But it should be done every day.) When it becomes easy to do this on any unfamiliar but simple piece, it will be no longer necessary.

---

[*] Any beginning method book, early Bach or similiar anthology, that has a single line per hand (at first) is suitable.

2) Pitches and Fingering Alone

- Observe only the pitch and fingering information in the piece.

- We will not attempt to play in time here. (In fact, this will be impossible!)

- TALK! — Verbalize every single pitch and finger that you see and play, one by one. Do this *before* (not *during*) each key stroke. (Speaking before playing promotes thinking before doing, a desired technique for what's going to come!) Say "G-5, F-2, E-1," etc.

- Say any vertically aligned notes (letter and finger number) from lowest to highest. *Then* play together.

- Hold each note until the next note is played.

- This drill forces you to become conscious of every single pitch. It is even more painfully dull than the **Rhythm Alone** drill. Again, don't do this one more than two minutes a day. But do it *every* day until it becomes easy.

The above two drills are only tools to enhance proper thinking. They do a fantastic job if you can tolerate them. Because they are so boring, again, don't do them more than the recommended short time each day. This will promote needed concentration and will avoid fatigue. (Best of both worlds!)

The purpose of verbalizing the above two drills is to bring the conscious awareness into play. You will reach a point where it becomes easier to do them without talking at all and that will probably be when these drills become no longer necessary. When you reach this stage, you'll know it's time to combine rhythm, pitches and fingering and to begin making music.

Howard's Rhythm Drill

This drill is to help show you how rhythms are superimposed over an ongoing pulse. Instructions for this are explained in the "Rhythm Alone" **Basic Perception Drills** (preceding). Play on any note. Say beat numbers and "ands" throughout.

Say: "1 & 2 & 3 & 4 &..."

4 The Process of Sight-Reading

Have you ever experienced the "let down" when you find out how a magic trick is really done? Didn't you secretly hope that the magician really *did* have some kind of super-human power and you were lucky to even stand next to him? Well, I don't want to disappoint you, but the process of sight-reading can be broken down into logical components that are quite ordinary. But working together, it is the *result* that can be extraordinary.

By addressing each element of the sight-reading process separately, it is then possible to find the weakness(es). Once we know where the problem is, it is easy to fix it. This is only a more specific application of the "find-the-problem-and-attack-it" philosophy of practice as proposed in the introduction. In other words, "the chain is only as strong as its weakest link."

The sight-reading chain can be reduced to the following:

1)	**Visual**	(eyes)	*see the notes*
	↓		
2)	**Electro/Chemical**	(nerves)	*think*
	↓		
3)	**Kinetic**	(muscles)	*play the notes*
	↓		
4)	**Aural**[*]	(ears)	*listen*

What we have here is simply a transfer of energy from one manifestation to another. In a good reader, it happens so fast that the steps blur as one. Even though this is so, trust that this sequence remains intact.

[*] Some people may wish to place the **Aural** step before the **Kinetic** because they feel that it is important to hear the sound in their mind's ear before it is played. Indeed, this is helpful but not essential.

Howard's Sight-Reading Drill

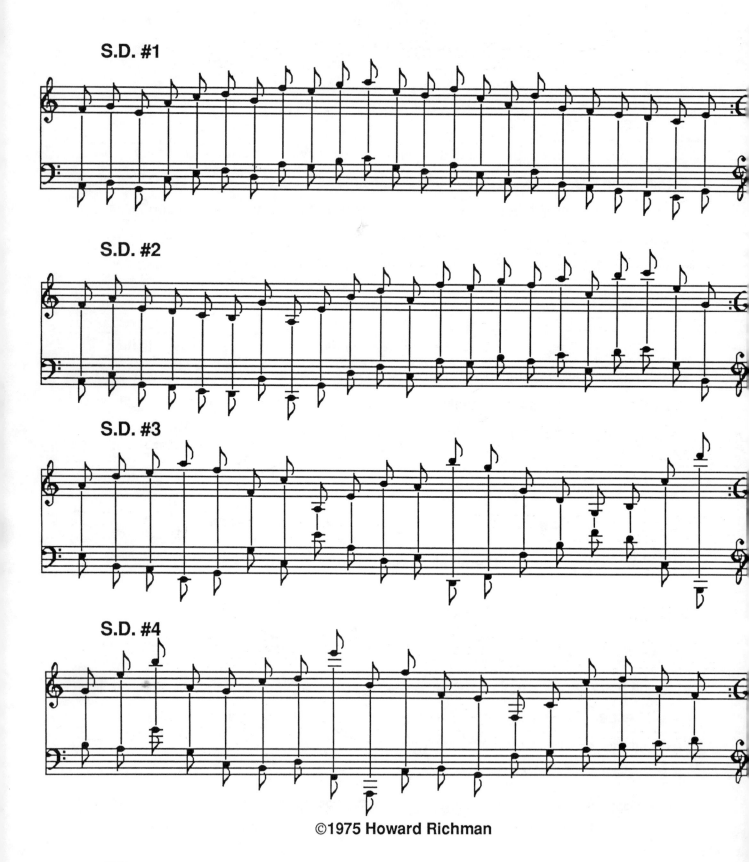

S.D. #1

S.D. #2

S.D. #3

S.D. #4

©1975 Howard Richman

Howard's Sight-Reading Drill
—Chromatic Alterations —

©1979 Howard Richman

Actually, with the steps being symbolized by the numbers, a more accurate model would look like this:

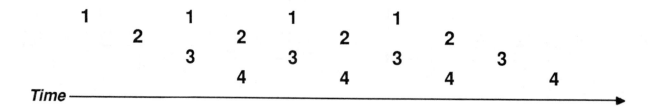

This shows that the steps must overlap for each sequence in order for a flow to occur. In other words, while we play one thing, we're looking at the next. **Looking ahead is an essential part of sight-reading.**

Although each of the 4 steps are vital to solid sight-reading ability, the drills to follow (Chapters 5 & 6) focus only on steps 1 and 3. It is beyond the scope of this book to discuss in detail steps 2 and 4, but I cannot emphasize their importance enough. They must be mastered in a more indirect manner and I urge you to allow for their concurrent improvement. Here's what I recommend:

Step 2: Electro/Chemical

This depends largely on your general state of health. Take the time to learn all you can about your physical and emotional heath. Thought processes and abilities depend on our various bodily systems (circulatory, respiratory, excretory, etc.) And these are intimately connected to the food we eat, our physical activity and our emotional state. To play the piano well is no easy task. Treat your body *at least* as well as an athlete would!

Step 4: Aural
Our ears are helpful to us in two ways:

A)   Hearing a note *before* we play it (in our head), by relative or absolute pitch, *can* help our fingers to go to the correct note.

B) Hearing a note *after* we play, allows us to check for mistakes and make subtle adjustments in dynamics of notes that follow.

Traditional ear-training is about the best thing you can do to develop your hearing. **Don't avoid it !!!**

Bringing our attention now to steps 1 and 3 (**Visual** and **Kinetic**), let's call them by names that are less clinical: *See* and *Play*. The next two chapters will focus on just this — maximizing what we see and making it easy to play. Chapter 5, **Keyboard Orientation Drills**, will free the player from having to constantly look down at his or her hands. This allows more visual contact with the notes, reduces getting lost, and makes it easier to look ahead. Chapter 6, **Visual Perception Drills**, will increase the player's information absorption rate.

These two sets of drills are explained separately for clarity but should be mastered simultaneously. The **Sight-Reading Program Matching Schedule** (following) will be helpful to pace yourself. Try to adjust your practice to insure that at all stages each **K.O. Drill** is linked with its respective **V.P. Drill**. Also, before going on, make sure you can easily do the **Basic Perception Drills** at the end of Chapter 3.

Sight-Reading Program Matching Schedule

Try to link the **Keyboard Orientation (K.O.) Drills** with the respective level **Visual Perception (V.P.) Drills** at all levels of your progress. If you excel in one area, then temporarily practice the corresponding drill even more. This will insure a fast and unified improvement. It can take anywhere from three months to four years to really get through the entire **K.O.** and **V.P.** set. Work hard but never force. Go at your own rate. Patience is best.

Drills labeled *a* are not variants of the numbered drills that precede them. The reason for identifying them in this way is simply to insure that they would be done during the same period of time.

K.O. #1	**V.P. #1**
K.O. #2	**V.P. #2**
K.O. #3	**V.P. #3**
K.O. #4	**V.P. #4**
K.O. #5, K.O. #5a	**V.P. #5, V.P. #5a**
K.O. #6	**V.P. #6, V.P. #6a**
K.O. #7	**V.P. #7, V.P. #7a**
K.O. #8 **K.O.#8a**	**V.P. #8, V.P. #8a**
K.O. #9	**V.P. #9, V.P. #9a**

Please Note: The **K.O.** and **V.P. Drills** make up the core of the program. In general, it is recommended that these be mastered *before* actually sight-reading (see Chapter 7) but this is not to deter you from regularly "testing" yourself by reading unfamiliar music in the meantime. The bulk of your sight-reading practice time, however, should be applied to the drills until you reach level 9. This will insure development of good habits.

5 Keyboard Orientation Drills

The best sight-readers rarely need to look at their hands. They have an intimate knowledge of every key. Also, blind pianists seem to do fine with their "obstacle." In developing the following drills, my intention was to artificially induce in myself what I observed to be natural or naturally-acquired in others.

The value for you in gaining a better sense of touch on your instrument not only will free your visual field to read music more easily (you won't have to keep looking down), but this "tactile" confidence will help you as a performer. For example, the singer/pianist will clearly benefit as he or she, being less bound to the keyboard, can relate better with the audience.

The K.O. Drills will indirectly help with finger technique. As you gain knowledge of key locations and begin thinking in groups of notes, you'll find that scales and arpeggios lie beneath the hand naturally. (Melodic passages contain either steps or skips, the components of scales and arpeggios. The better we can play scales and arpeggios, the better we can play anything.)

Let's divide our sense of touch at the keyboard into two general areas: **referential** and **absolute.**

The **referential** sense of touch is based on how well we would identify a note by *looking* at it. Realize that we only know a note is called "D" because of its position within the 2 black notes. The same will be true for *feeling* the keys: find the "D" by first feeling for the 2 blacks that surround it. Make a clear imprint in your mind: the C, D, and E belong to the 2 blacks, and the F, G, A, and B belong to the 3 blacks. We should be able to find any note in "reference" to the one we just played.

The **absolute** sense of touch is a little less obvious, but just as important. Sometimes a passage calls for jumping great distances where we cannot "refer" to the previous note by touch. In this situation, we must rely on our absolute sense awareness of the key location. This will develop gradually in many people by chance, but that's not good enough for us. Make your resolution right now to *always* sit in the exact same place at the keyboard. This will encourage a physiological memory of where the keys are in relation to your body. The exact center of the piano keyboard is between E and F. Instead of sitting there, I recommend that you sit at "middle D." Getting microscopic, you should not only sit at middle D but your belly button should be in the *middle* of middle D. Now you will have the benefit of perfect symmetry to balance both sides of your brain, enhancing the tactile memory for each. If you play instruments with various keyboard lengths, still sit (or stand) at D. You can always *lean* left and right, but don't change your base (don't scoot).

The following drills will develop both the referential and the absolute senses of touch. They are all to be done without looking at the hands (except at first). Don't forget that the **Visual Perception (V.P.) Drills** in the next chapter are to be done concurrently to the **K.O. Drills**, not afterwards. (See **Sight-Reading Program Matching Schedule**.) As weird as any of these drills may seem, **don't take it upon yourself to skip over any of them**. They have been carefully arranged in sequence and tested successfully. Each step prepares you for the level to follow.

K.O. Drill # 1

Learn to play the 2 and 3 black keys on the keyboard without looking at your hands. Both hands move in parallel, playing the identical group, one octave apart. *Feel* with the flattest and most flexible fingers possible as your hands bump and glide into the new position. This sensitizes more skin surface area than just the tips. (Let the keys touch the bottom of your fingers, lodge between the fingers and even the palm area.) Be sure to keep the fingers parallel to the keys at all times. Now, after arriving at each new black group, *curve* the fingers, not by pushing the hand deeper into the keys, but by pulling the fingers toward you so that the last joint is in a vertical position on each black note. (Place the 2nd and 3rd fingers on the two blacks and the 2nd, 3rd, and 4th fingers on the three blacks.) Now *play* that group as a cluster, using the weight if your arm rather than the finger muscles. Repeat for each group. Condensed, this drill is:

1) **Feel Flat**
2) **Curve**
3) **Play**
4) **Repeat on next black group**, ascending and descending

K.O. Drill # 2

The first white note above each black group is E and B. The first white note below each black group is F and C. Keeping the fingers now in the curved position only, play either E and B or F and C with the thumb as a pivot between each group.

Example:

Play	2 blacks →	E →	3 blacks →	B →	2 blacks →	etc.
with fingers	2,3	1	2,3,4	1	2,3	

Try to keep the hand shallow enough in the key bed that the thumb can reach its notes from the front edge. This will reduce the need to pop the wrist up and down or left and right. The hand should remain quiet while the thumb stretches. This is not easy to do at first without looking because of the tendency to over- or under-shoot the thumb in one hand or the other. Practice a small portion at a time and gradually you should be able to do this on the entire keyboard with both hands together without looking — on B,E and F,C each, up and down. Aside from enhancing your relative sense of touch, this drill is preparing you for the correct blocking out of scales.

K.O. Drill # 3

If you play the **K.O. Drill #2** note by note and start on B for the B/E set, and Db for the C/F set, you end up with the B and Db major scales! These 2 scales are the best to learn first because of the way they lie under the hands. If you learn to shift properly from hand to thumb in these configurations, all the other major and minor scales will be easy. So, **K.O. #3** is simply to practice, without looking, the B and Db major scales. Begin slowly, stretching the thumbs beneath the hands. Eventually, be able to play 4 octaves up and down at a rapid pace.

K.O. Drill # 4

It's time to play triads without looking. First, a mini-theory lesson on chord construction:

Chords are made of 3rds, and 3rds are made of 2nds. So let's review:

Minor 2nd: (half step): the smallest possible interval on the keyboard

Major 2nd: (whole step): two half steps

Minor 3rd: (whole + half step)

Major 3rd: (two whole steps)

Learn the above and experiment picking out intervals at the keyboard. Mastery of 2nds and 3rds is crucial to your understanding of chords.

Chord — defined as 3 or more notes arranged by 3rds

Triad — a chord with only three notes

The four kinds of triads are:

Major = M3 + m3 (Major 3rd [M3] with a Minor 3rd [m3] on top)

Minor = m3 + M3

Diminished = m3 + m3

Augmented = M3 + M3

Now, here's the drill part: On every note of the chromatic scale, ascending and descending, play the following chords: Major, Minor, Diminished, Augmented, Major, in root position (no doublings) in both hands (with any fingers), without looking. Say the name of each chord **before** you play it.

Example: say	"C Major"	play
	"C Minor"	play
	"C Diminished"	play
	"C Augmented"	play
	"C Major"	play

Then do the same on C♯, and continue to C, one octave higher. Then descend.

Identify the chords starting on the black notes by their sharp names going up and by their flat names going down. This will help you recognize them either way and become familiar with them. Soon, you may notice a pattern of changes as you go from one chord to the next. For example, from major to minor, the middle note of the chord moves down by half step.

K.O. Drill # 5

In preparation for arpeggios, which are nothing more than rolled chords, learn the 3 inversions of all major and minor chords, doubling the bass note. Even though it admittedly is awkward in many situations, I urge you to follow the suggested fingering in the example below and to maintain that (per inversion) for *every* key, major or minor. It will *save* thought-time later. This is an intelligent compromise. Each chord in one hand has its layout in "reverse" in the other. This relation is shown by the dotted lines.

Example: (shown for the key of C major, but fingering is identical for all keys, major or minor)

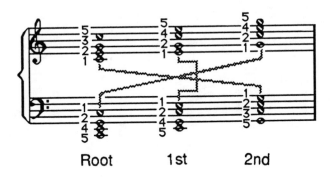

Root   1st   2nd

Be able to ascend and descend chromatically, without looking (eventually) on all 3 inversions. Master them in this order only: 1) Root positions, 2) 2nd inversions, *then* 3) 1st inversions. Say the name of each chord before you play it and be aware of which finger(s) will be playing the root.

K.O. Drill # 5a

Get a book of all the major and minor scales. Begin practicing all 24 major and minor keys. Note how every key is similiar to the B and Db major scales. Every key has a group of 3 + 4 notes per hand. They may start mid-sequence and coincide at different places, but you now have the right digital preparation needed to do this. Eventually be able to play every scale 4 octaves up and down, without looking. Plan to continue playing scales for the rest of your life.

K.O. Drill # 6

Now that you can play chords in any inversion of any key, pick one or two keys a day and shift, without looking, up and down the whole keyboard, staying in the key.

The sequence is: Root-1st-2nd-Root-1st-2nd-etc..., then reverse. Later, practice rolling these chords and you have instant arpeggios. Begin working in a key that has a black note in it. This gives you something to grab on to.

K.O. Drill # 7

This is an "octave displacement " drill. Be able to do it on every inversion of every chord used in **K.O. #6**. The purpose of this is to develop your leap judgment without looking. You will be trading fingers (pivoting) 1-5 and 5-1. Go up in parallel, back, contrary, and back for each chord-shape practiced.

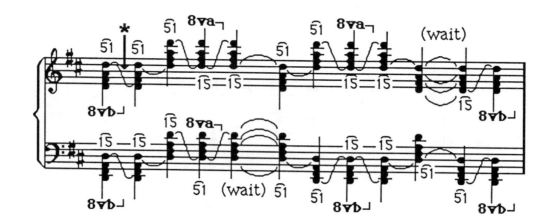

The essence of this drill is that you hold finger 5 down while you trade it with 1, and vice versa in the other direction. (Please note ties in the above example, indicating a pivot between fingers. The first tie is marked by an asterisk [*].)

K.O Drill #8

Do the same as in **K.O. #7**, but without the pivot and (therefore) without the hand contraction. Just keep your hand formed to the chord played and glide it gently to the next octave, without looking. Remember the approximate distance, as determined by the pivot in **K.O. #7**. Also, allow the fingers to slide along and "drop" into the right place when they get there. Each chord has a special feel. Sensitize yourself to this now.

K.O. Drill # 8a

Play the exercise as shown below on every pitch. Be aware that this is just outlining a sequence of octaves and these may be felt more clearly if you detect the (major?) chord each octave could suggest.

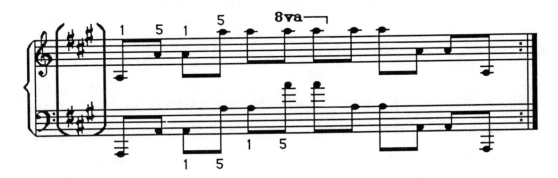

K.O Drill # 9

Do the same as in **K.O. #8,** but place the hands on your lap between chords (similiar to **V.P. #8**). Eventually, to make it a little harder, instead of placing the hand on your lap, throw them wildly into the air and turn your head from left to right. This should simulate playing a piece with leaps while looking at the conductor (or fellow musician) and back — *without* losing your place or otherwise goofing up. If you can do this, YOU PASS!

6 Visual Perception Drills

Please make sure you can do the **Basic Perception Drills** as described in Chapter 3 before beginning the series of **Visual Perception Drills**. (It is possible that **V.P. #1** *only* can be done as a preparation for the Basic Perception Drills.)

Of the three primary elements of written music we need to perceive, this chapter will focus on pitch and fingering recognition. For *rhythm* perception training, the best thing you can do is to continue saying the beats of any piece you play as you play it, This can be done with "dummy" notes (Chapter 3) or with the correct pitches.

The first few **V.P. Drills** work with *Howard's Sight-Reading Drill* (see book center). You will go through these drills several times, doing something more advanced each time. The notes in **Sight Drills (S.D.) #1** and **#2** are arranged in parallel. This can function as a self-check: If you say the same note for treble and bass, you know you're wrong. **Drill #3** deals with the mirror image, which can be confusing for some people. **Drill #4** is random.

Later drills will use Bach Chorales. When buying these, be sure to get the "keyboard" version which has 2 notes per staff. (The choral version has one note per staff, but *four* staves!)

V.P. Drill # 1

Using *Howard's Sight-Reading Drill*, practice just saying the notes out loud (no playing). Stay on **S.D. #1** until you can say each note in succession at an average speed of 1 second per note. Then go to the next drill. Follow this rule until you get to

S.D. #4. The lines connecting the treble and bass staves are only to assist wandering (lost) eyes. Always read from the bottom to the top, *then* go on. This will train the eye to see the bass first on any vertical combination, which will be helpful later in terms of grasping the harmony. **If you need help identifying the note, please refer to Chapter 3 for an in-depth explanation of an effective process.**

Say each note with a short monotone voice. Don't say "A?, B?" (with an ascending tone to your voice). This projects doubt, and takes energy away from thinking. This is picky, I know, but trust me.

Make sure you flip the page upside down for more variety. You will be done with **V.P. Drill #1** when you can say **S.D. #4** at an average speed of 1 note per second. (Don't attempt to do **S.D. #5-8** until you reach the advanced drills.)

V.P. Drill # 2

Return to **S.D. #1**, but now *play* each note after you say it — and *do* look at your hands. Follow these guides carefully: Keep your hands on your lap until they are needed to play a note. Then return them instantly to your lap. This forces you to find each note fresh. Don't say the note while you play it. Say it *before*. **Don't move your hand in the direction of the note until you say it.** (You think this saves time but it does the reverse!) Here's the simplified sequence:

1) **Say Note**

2) **Find the right key** with your eyes *only*

3) **Move Hand Quickly** to play it

4) **Go to Next Note**

It is *crucial* that you make these steps distinct at this stage. Don't try to go fast yet. Rather, learn the correct procedure with confidence and relaxation. Speed will surely follow. I guarantee: *Every* time you play a wrong note or have a hesitation, it's because you overlapped the suggested sequence (Because you're in a hurry?) and it just cancels out your brain! Your brain can only do one thing at a time, yet each may be done at the rate of microseconds, giving the illusion of many things at once. If you actually try to *do* many things at once, *nothing* happens. Try it! (I refer to conscious awareness in the above statement. Obviously these are a multitude of automatic *subconscious* bodily functions that occur very nicely in a simultaneous manner.)

If you go about this exactly as I say and you *still* have hesitation, it's probably because you keep losing your place. The solution to this is to mentally notice the shape and position ("2nd space, bass") of the note you just said before you look down to play it. When you look back up to the page, look first for *this* note and then quickly move your eyes to the next. The problem usually is that (in our "hurry") we try to look back up at the next note but we don't know what the next note is!

Progress numerically from **S.D. #1** to **#4** only when you can do each stage at the rate of one second per note.

V.P. Drill # 3

I think it's a crime for piano teachers to block the view of their students' hands with a book in their effort to "teach" them to play without looking. If, however, the student were taught first what to feel *for*, then this would make sense.

Well, it just so happens that having done the **K.O. Drills** (Chapter 5) thus far, you have been "touch-sensitized" and you're now ready to play **Sight-Drill #1** without looking! Remember, we never feel for the white note itself — we feel for the surrounding group of blacks, and then, in reference, can locate the note in question.

Prepare by saying the name of the note, and then saying what black group it belongs to (2's or 3's). For example: "A......3's." Feel for the 3's and play the A with the closest finger. Easy! Eventually you won't need to speak at all because the process will become automatic. At this stage however, speaking out loud will promote thinking in the most efficient sequence. Please refer to **Keyboard Boundaries** in Chapter 3 to clarify how to determine *which* 2's or 3's is the right one. Be sure to place your hands back on your lap each time to create a fresh discovery of each note. This is now getting into the **absolute** sense of touch. Progress through **Sight Drills #1-#4** when you achieve a one-second-each average, as before, but now without looking at your hands. Remember to always sit in the same place (middle D). If you don't, these drills will lose much of their impact.

An effective variant of this drill will be to play each note four times each, directly from your lap after saying it once. Make sure you don't merely jump up to the note itself with each repetition. Rather, allow other fingers to touch or bump the nearest black note(s). This is because you're practicing not how to play the note but how to *feel for* the note. You'll find that the first note played may be slower. Each successive repetition, however, will be faster. This is the immediate memory working. After several days or weeks, the immediate memory becomes long-term memory and you will be able to locate the note the first time as fast as the last! Also, be sure to divorce your conscious awareness from your hand during the repetitions. Take advantage of this "extended" time to be reading the *next* note. Later, when you go back to one time each, you will appreciate your new ability to play one note while looking at the next.

V.P. Drill # 4

Progress through **S.D. #1-4** without looking as before, but now with both hands playing together.

Proper Sequence:
1) **Say** the bass then the treble note
2) From lap, try to **feel** for these two notes *at the same time* (Not one after the other)
3) **Play** together — Place hands on lap
4) **Repeat** on next set

It again will be helpful to occasionally play each set four times each.

V.P. Drill # 5

We are now completely done with *Howard's Sight-Reading Drill.* (Hooray!!) After a brief moment of unrestrained jubilation, get out your Bach Chorales and notice that there are two notes (generally) per staff. Observing only the main beats (not the "ands"), play them hands alternating (L-R-L-R) without looking. You no longer need to say the names of the notes out loud (Hooray Again!) Don't forget to return your hands to your lap after each one. Since we are now playing more than one note per hand, realize that we are no longer feeling for the 2 and 3 blacks in their pure form. Try now to be sensitive to more subtle geographic contours between black and white keys. Learn what different intervals feel like (3rds, 4ths).

The four times variant is excellent here. Get a bookmark and save your place. Never do the same Chorale again until you've done them all.

V.P. Drill # 5a

While you're doing the "removing hands" method in **V.P. #5**, you also want to play the Bach Chorales *legato*. Hands alone, with *or* without looking at your hands (it doesn't matter), play *every* note. Although it is sometimes impossible, try to connect each note as smoothly to the next as possible. You will need to learn how to "trade fingers" now. This means while the key is still being depressed, trade it with another finger (if necessary) which will be more advantageous for the note(s) that follow. This is a marvelous way to learn to look and to think ahead. Don't try to play in tempo at this point.

V.P. Drill # 6

Same as **V.P. Drill #5**, but now try it hands together.

V.P. Drill # 6a

Same as **V.P. Drill #5a**, but now play legato with both hands simultaneously.

V.P. Drill # 7

Displace octaves now on each main beat in the Bach Chorales. First, go in a mirrored direction and then in parallel, as shown in the example below. Repeat the same sequence with every main beat in the Bach Chorales. Glide hands on the keyboard as you shift from one position to the next. Feel the "terrain" of the notes as the hands gently fall into place. It's always best to master this and any other drill by first trying hands separately.

Example:

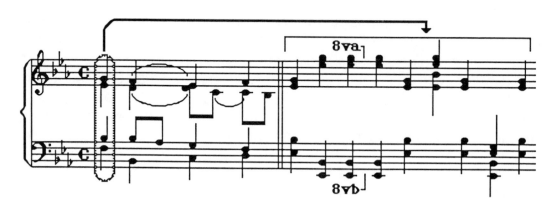

V.P. Drill # 7a

Play every note of the Bach Chorales hands alone, without looking, one octave displaced. This means play the whole left hand one octave below what is written, and the right hand one octave above what is written, throughout. Keep each hand on the keyboard at all times but don't necessarily feel obligated to play legato. This can be suprisingly disorienting at first. Don't worry. This expands the relative sense of touch awareness, which has by now become stale. A variation would be to do it two octaves displaced.

V.P. Drill # 8

Do exactly the same as **V.P. #7**, but between each position place your hands on your lap and then return to the *next* position. This will take some practice but when you get it, you will have had a tremendous breakthrough! (Don't expect to jump to the correct notes exactly. Rather, get to the general area, then feel.)

V.P. Drill # 8a

The same as **V.P. #7a**, but now hands together.

V.P. Drill # 9

Same as **V.P. #8**, but with the "mix up" approach as described in **K.O. #9**.

V.P. Drill # 9a

Play the Bach Chorales in the normal register, leaving hands on the keys, legato, without looking at the hands, and up to tempo. Congratulations! You've concluded the formal part of this program.

7 _Now_ You're Ready !

If you can sight-read Bach Chorales up to tempo, which already make good use of the keyboard register, you are definitely on your way. _Now_ I recommend: "sight-read every day." _Now_ you have the foundation that will be self-improving. You will avoid practicing bad habits.

There are two different approaches, each of which you should take:

1) **Play easy pieces up to tempo.** Force yourself to keep going no matter what. Don't worry about mistakes. This helps you to look ahead.
2) **Play difficult pieces super slowly.** Don't dare make even one mistake. This helps to develop accuracy.

Get in the habit of looking at the meter and key signature before you begin playing. You may now use a metronome to pace yourself, or it is now a good time to begin playing with other musicians. Try now, not only to churn out the notes, but also to pick up other subtleties on the first reading, such as tempo and dynamic changes.

Be adventurous with your "practice" pieces. Don't sight-read music only in your preferred musical style. Diversify. Need practice reading scales? Look at Mozart. How are your leaps in the left hand? Try ragtime. Above all, you've _done_ the dirty work. From now on you can improve and have fun too!

8 Advanced Drills

Even though you will now improve substantially by merely sight-reading, it is still possible to intentionally boost any lingering weaknesses by doing specific exercises. I list several here that have helped me in various ways. They are not in any particular order. You may choose to do or to *not* do any of them. Also, feel free to devise your own.

- **Take a look at the *Chromatic Sight-Reading Drill*,** book center.

- **Obtain music intended for single-clef instruments** (flute, bass clarinet, etc.) **and play it with one hand very fast.** Etudes written for that instrument are perfect. This develops *horizontal* perception (looking ahead).

- **Have a friend cover up music with a card *as you play.*** The catch here is that you are to play the music that was just covered up! What this does is to force your short-term photographic memory to wake up. If you think about it, that is what sight-reading is — memorizing, even for an instant, and then playing it back. Of course, the rate of "cover-up" will vary, depending on your ability and the difficulty of the piece. This approach is one of the standard "methods" of improving one's sight-reading. It will also contribute to your *horizontal* perception.

- **Practice all kinds of finger technique, and pieces you already know, without looking at your hands.** A creative way to do this is to play in the dark. This will add confidence to your sense of touch.

- **Read string quartets** (you'll have to learn alto clef), **choral music, organ preludes, or even orchestral scores.** Practice very slowly and learn to condense what you see into your mortal two hands. This develops *vertical* perception.

- **Look for patterns in music.** Don't be afraid to look way ahead for a second just so you can anticipate what will be easy or difficult. Patterns are easy. If you detect a pattern then you can devote your concentration to other things.

- **Special rhythm drills** and other musical tricks can be invaluable. Get a book like Hindemith's *Elementry Training for Musicians* and use it. A partner may be helpful for this.

- **Develop your chord-reading ability.** I mean this in two ways. The obvious way refers to chord symbols written above piano/vocal scores (Cm7, G9, etc.) There are many books and teachers available to help you with this. The second way, which is dependent on the first, deals with being able to grasp the harmony of a passage at a glance. This technique may be best acquired with the score and a pencil, away from the keyboard. This will be helpful in your "faking" ability. Now don't misunderstand me, I don't want you to be dishonest. But, part of being a good sight-reader is absorbing necessary information as fast as possible. Sometimes it's safer to fake a G minor chord than to try to read every single note and blow it.

- **Increasing Intervallic Octave-Jumping Exercise.** With double octaves (one octave per hand), select a note as a *home base,* then gradually increase the distance of the notes jumped to, below and above, without looking. Each day, select a different starting note.

    Example: (shown on a single note but to be done with octaves)

- **Practice the chord-shifting drills** (See later K.O. Drills) **but with chords other than triads.** Try diminished, 7th, 9th, and even "Jazz chord" clusters.

- **Transposing at sight** is one of the most confusing things of all. This can come in handy, however, and you may wish to prepare for the need. Slowly master the two following approaches to this technique and they will eventually merge as one.

    A) First decide what is the intervallic shift. (Transposing the key of G major up to Bb major would be up a minor 3rd or down a major 6th. Up a minor third is closer, therefore easier.) Look at every single note (or chord if you're reading chords) and play the note (or chord) that would be this very interval away. You'll have to go *very* slowly. Don't rush it.

    B) After deciding the intervallic shift, apply method "A" for the first note only. Thereafter, notice the intervallic distance between every note (or chord) that follows from the one you're playing. Simply shift the identical distance but in reference to the one you just played rather than the one that is written. The problem with this method is that if you goof once, all the rest will be wrong — but don't give up.

9 Contemporary Classical Music

Whether you like the sound of it or not, contemporary music is great fun to play, especially with other people, and it can really stretch your reading ability in a hurry. Rule #1: Never say no if someone invites you to accompany them in a "modern" piece.

Since there often is an "equalizing" formula for the pitches in this music, there is great opportunity for expression in the realm of dynamics and rhythm. *This* is where you should place your consideration. See how quickly you can pick up the subtle dynamic indications, as they constantly change in much of this music. Rhythmically, contemporary music can be quite confusing. I recommend drawing light vertical lines with a pencil through the main beats (if you have time to practice it.) Then if you get lost, you can always quickly align yourself with the appropriate beat.

If you allow for it, you should find in some ways that contemporary music can be even easier to read than traditional repertoire. (Of course, this is not always true.) Not that I suggest faking, but since it's harder to tell if there is a mistake, I find that my "wrong-note-anxiety" disappears and I end up playing even *more* accurately! Not only that, but this extra confidence carries over when returning to traditional music. See if this happens to you.

10 Applications to Other Instruments

Although this book is written with the keyboard player in mind, it is easily adapted to players of other instruments. The sense-of-touch and visual perception principles are universal. Each instrument will provide its own challenges in these areas. For example, orientation on the flute is virtually no problem because the fingers stay pretty well in the same place. On the other hand, it is a special challenge for the percussionist, whose point of reference keeps changing. Also, visual perception will vary in difficulty according to the instrument. The cello may be written between three clefs, whereas the tympani may only use two *notes* at a time.

If you play an instrument other than keyboard and you have a reading weakness, use a little cleverness in applying these concepts to your obstacles. For example, it is possible for a vibes player to stand in one place and develop a spatial memory. A non-fretted string instrument could be temporarily adapted with tape "bumps" on the back to serve as musical "training wheels." As far as the **Visual Perception Drills** are concerned, if your instrument deals with only one clef, then practice the sight-drills in that clef only. Being a pianist, I am not intimately aware of the reading difficulties on all other instruments. However, if the least that this book does is to inspire you to make up special exercises for *your* instrument, I feel that I've succeeded.

11 On Your Own

I want to remind you to be patient with yourself. Follow this program carefully and trust that you will improve at the pace that is right for you.

Be confident. Your body language influences the reality. Even under pressure, stay calm. If you feel like you can't read up to the demand of the situation, either quit or *act* as if you can (pretend) and you'll see that this will help. Learn to feel that your instrument is your friend, that it is even a *part* of you.

The better you sight-read, the better you'll play and the more enjoyment you'll receive. Let me know how you come along. I'm interested in both your success stories and in any suggestions or special problems you have. And please remember this: You deserve to take a guilt-free day off once in a while. Work hard at this program but don't forget to enjoy yourself.

If you've enjoyed this book, you may be interested in other books and tapes offered by Sound Feelings Publishing. We specialize in the music, education, and health-related fields. Our tapes contain a unique type of "music for emotions" such as our *Feeling Stressed* and *Feeling Fat* tapes.

New books and tapes are in development. Write for a current catalog.

Sound Feelings Publishing
Suite 44
24266 Walnut Street
Newhall, California   91321
U.S.A.